In-Vision My Beauty

A Practical Guide to Give You Beauty from Ashes

Rohesia Hicks

In-Vision My Beauty: A Practical Guide to Give You Beauty from Ashes by *Rohesia Hicks*
Published by *ThroneRoom Expressions*
ThroneRoom Expressions Publishing Headquarters
33 Old Mill Lane
Southampton, PA 18966

©2024 Rohesia Hicks. All rights reserved. No part of this publication may be reproduced, stored in a retrieval system or transmitted in any form by any means, mechanical, electronic, photocopying, recording or otherwise – without the prior written permission of the author.

Cover Design by *ThroneRoom Expressions* & *Addison Graphics*
Editing by *ThroneRoom Expressions*.

For more information please contact:
ThroneRoom Expressions Publishing
throneroomexpressions@gmail.com.

Library of Congress Control Number: *2024919335*

Printed in the United States

www.visionsofbelle.org

DEDICATION

To my granny Catherine "Isa" Simon and my mommy, Jacinta Hicks, you are my strength. My sisters Shireen and Tiara, you always have my back. My ROD-Trina and Ms. Pam, you both have always supported me without question. My godchildren and to the Belles and future Belles that will come.

Table of Contents

Dedication……………………………………….…..3

Preface…………………………………….....……..5

Foreword………………………………………....…..8

CHAPTER 1: Get Ready!………………………..13

CHAPTER 2: Path Less Traveled………..…….…25

CHAPTER 3: You Have Arrived…………….……35

CHAPTER 4: Ring My Belle…………………...…49

CHAPTER 5: Was I Dreaming?……………..……..58

CHAPTER 6: Where's My Return………..….……64

FINALE: I AM Affirmations…………..…………..71

PREFACE

Growing up, I was a girl that always stood out. I was outspoken, bubbly and social. My mom always told me that she would pray over me so much because she knew I was different. She knew there was something special about me unlike any other girl. She strived to keep me close because, with precious cargo, you must keep it secured and very close. Little did she know that with all the prayers and precautions, a thing called life would interfere with that safety net. I would be faced with attacks from people near and far that would ultimately shake the confidence and boldness incorporated in my innocence.

I grew up during the time when people were always telling my peers and I who we should be and how we should act. No one ever mentioned how to become that woman. As women, we battle with so much, and it can feel very overwhelming and beyond draining. They tell us to be less emotional, stop being so angry, and how we need to know our place. We should be seen and not heard. Let me be the first to tell you, if you haven't already been told, that is straight foolishness!

As children we are raised by an adult that should have spoken life into us and taught us right from wrong. These adults are supposed to make us feel safe and protect us from all danger seen and unseen. Unfortunately for us they also were not taught how to.

If we took a poll, by the age of 12 years old, 1 out of 4 girls will have experienced some type of trauma, loss, abandonment, or some form of abuse. Even worse, they will not receive adequate guidance to maneuver through the matter so that they can be empowered and have the reinforcements they need to understand that it wasn't their fault. Similar to a wound that goes untreated; it is susceptible to an infection that can eventually lead to deterioration when untreated.

When a young girl has been *"infected"* negative thoughts take hold and grow. This is why I felt writing this book was needed. This is not meant to replace therapy or be the end all be all to you getting your healing.
Becoming a woman of greatness is not something that happens with a click of a heel. Throughout these chapters I will share how I navigated through the smoke and mirrors. I will share how I often felt I wasn't good enough, that I was out of place and second guessed who I was and what I brought to places.

For every form of abuse you may have been subjected to, every trauma you experienced and every negative word spoken to you or over your life, I want you to know it was and is not your fault! I cannot erase what happened or wave a magic wand so that you will be healed from it. I wish I could.

The sole purpose of this book is to share how I have navigated through the process that people don't always tell us or are too ashamed to share. It was created to assist by building and empowering you to be the best version of yourself so that you can learn how to move from your current state to a more healthy and desired state of mind. As you read, remember that regardless of your past or present circumstance, you too can be the lady that stands out from the rest.

Now Miss Lady, straighten your crown and boldly walk in the authority that you were birthed with by taking your rightful place at the table you created. You are deserving and worthy of it and so much more!

FOREWORD

The Beauty of the Journey Ahead:

I met Ro through our mutual mentor, Roni, and we connected instantly. She saw me. But it was deeper than that. She dealt with the future version of me while our friendship blossomed in the present. Truthfully, at the time, my faith was shattered. I had gone through a season of heartbreak, failure, and depression before meeting Ro. So, you can imagine how emotionally guarded I was. But we spent our first meeting laughing until our stomachs hurt, and it was one of the most refreshing exchanges I allowed myself to have. While sharing my hurt and brokenness, she asked me to be a keynote speaker for a conference. I told her NO y'all. I asked her to find someone else to do it. And if she could not, then she could call me as a backup plan. (I called it a "Hail Mary"). Well, Ro cashed in her Hail Mary, lol. God was dealing with me, reminding me I could be used even in brokenness.

Truthfully, God used Ro to prove it. Ro was further along on her journey, but she pulled over because she could see that I was at a fork in the road. All I needed was a reminder that GREATNESS WAS MY DESTINATION. For that reminder, I will forever be grateful for our sisterhood Ro. From that initial connection, I made professional strides as a leader in higher education, women's empowerment, and, more recently, fundraising and development. No matter what I accomplish, I keep God at the center, the love of family as support, and friends like Ro to remind me that I am destined for more than what I see today. I am honored to encourage you to read her first book, *In-Vision My Beauty*, because you will also connect with Ro as your sister-friend, reminding you of your GREATNESS!

To My Radiant Sisters on the Journey of Life,

Welcome to a guide that mirrors the essence of our spirits, our heart's rhythm, and our souls' journey and holds the transformative power to change your life. "In-Vision My Beauty" is more than a book; it is a compass for the soul, a beacon of light in moments of darkness, and a testament to the power of faith, resilience, and self-discovery. What sets this book apart is its unique blend of personal narrative, practical advice, and spiritual insights, making it a comprehensive guide for women seeking self-discovery, empowerment, and spiritual awakening.

This book unfolds the inspirational journey of Rohesia Hicks, a woman whose spirit is as unyielding as it is tender, whose faith is as profound as her questions, and whose path is marked by the beauty of transformation. Rohesia's story is not just a story; it is like a quilt woven with threads of determination, grace and an unwavering belief in the power of self-realization. Her journey, filled with challenges and triumphs, serves as a mirror reflecting the trek of every woman who dares to dream, to fight, and to grow.

If you have picked up this book, it is because you're on a quest—perhaps you're at a crossroads, seeking direction or yearning to uncover the fullest expression of your being. "In-Vision My Beauty" speaks to you, the woman in pursuit of her authentic self, the woman who knows that the journey is as significant as the destination.

Life's journey is akin to driving on a vast, unpredictable road. Let prayer and reflection be your rearview and side mirrors, offering glimpses of how far you have journeyed and revealing the unseen spaces that lie just beyond your sight. As you delve into these pages, I invite you to gaze through the windshield—your expansive and clear vision of the future, reminding you of the boundless possibilities ahead.

In-Vision My Beauty is more than a book; it's your personal GPS. It's a guide that will lead you to the ultimate destination: the best version of yourself. It underscores the profound truth that faith is our divine NAVIGATION system, a reminder that, though we may veer off course, we can RECALCULATE. Even in moments of uncertainty, when our path seems obscured, remember that recalibration is just a part of the journey. This book is here to support you, to AFFIRM your worth, and to illuminate the way to your DESTINATION.

As you gain momentum, drawing inspiration from Rohesia's resilience and wisdom, remember the legacy you are part of and the path you pave for those who will follow. Embrace the love and support of those who walk with you, and extend forgiveness where the journey diverges, knowing that each step forward is a step toward liberation and fulfillment.

In-Vision My Beauty is an invitation to embark on a profound journey of self-discovery, empowerment, and spiritual awakening. It is a call to embrace your power, navigate the roads of life with grace and courage, and become the beacon of light for yourself and the generations that will follow. The book delves into Rohesia's personal experiences, offering insights, lessons, and practical advice on overcoming challenges, finding inner strength, and discovering one's true beauty.

May God bless, keep, and show you the abundance of His love as you read this book. I encourage you to take the first step on your journey of self-discovery and empowerment as you read your copy of *In-Vision My Beauty, A Practical Guide to Give You Beauty from Ashes* today.

-Yolanda V. Jackson

Chapter 1
Get Ready!

Identify where you currently are at. You want to become the woman you desire to be before life hits you.

Beep, Beep, Beep (sounds go off). With one eye open and the other eye closed, you wildly search for your cell phone and shut the alarm off. Yes! You find it and wince at the brightness of the light from your cell phone. Just like second nature, as easy as you breathe in and out, you click on that social media app that you swear you will only be on for a few minutes because you have a full day ahead. Instantly you start to fall down the social media rabbit hole.

You first check to see the notifications and how many people liked your latest post. Then check out who has seen your story thus far. Ugh, only eight new likes. But 60 people have viewed my story, so it's not too bad. Now to check out my feed.

Bossybellesquotes: *"Be the leader you want to see."* Yessss, LIKE. Keep scrolling. The latest meme about some rappers. Keep scrolling. Ooooh. What is the Shameless Tea talking about? Rapper Lady S. puts out a diss track talking about her best friend (see prior post). Just like that, you click on the profile and start scrolling through their page and comments to piece the story together. You realize it's another story about celebrities beefing with each other, and think to yourself how women must do better and stop being at each other's throat. Scroll, scroll, go back to feed. Scroll, scroll, and see half-naked women with a nice round backside. Fake but nice. You start thinking about how you just need a shot in both butt cheeks to give you that plump round look. Or maybe you should just suck out all the fat in your stomach and put it in your butt because then you could look amazing like them. Way cuter of course. Scroll.

"*Alexa, what time is it?*"

"*It is 7:25 am.*"

You vow that you will only stay on IG (Instagram) for five more minutes, then get out of bed and start getting ready for the day. Still scrolling and its 20 minutes later. You look at this happy couple's post. They look so happy and in love. Ugh, God, where is my black love?

It is like everybody has someone, even the least attractive ones. Scrolling. O.M.Geeee. She got a new job, benefits, and incentives!! Ugh, how did she manage that? She used to copy off my work when we were in school. Let me like this post because I can't have her thinking I'm jealous. I'm no hater. Let me comment on her post;

"*Go girl, CONGRATS (party popper emoji).*"

Hmmmm. Now what should I post?

"*What's for you will always BE for you.*"

CAPTION: Don't compare yourself to others because it is not wise because what God has for you is FOR YOU!
Ooooh yeah. That's good. POSTED.

Ok, it's time to get up for real now. Sitting up on the edge of the bed, stretching and yawning, all the things that need to be accomplished run all through your mind. Dreading that today might be the last straw that broke the camel's back. Yesterday was long and draining. Today has to be better. Right?

You get up and head straight to the bathroom. Reaching for your toothbrush and toothpaste and stopping dead in your tracks. You stop because you have caught a glimpse of a young woman that some days you don't even recognize. You initially think it's because the mirror is a little dirty from the residue of toothpaste and hair products. You take a closer look. You are so close that you can see every pore on that milk chocolate, rich and creamy brown skin. You stare so hard and intensely that your dark almond-shaped brown eyes begin to get bigger. Your eyes are so fixated on the woman you are becoming. You don't even blink because you think you will miss something. Mirror, mirror on the wall, do you see what I see? Tell me the truth; am I all that you see? Am I the person that people have told me or what I convinced myself to be? I know people will tell me things that aren't true or what I want to hear. Shoot, I even tell myself false things but not this bathroom mirror. A mirror shows a reflection of an object or person that appears almost identical, but I continue to stare. This is not the time to just glance but zoom in so much that you feel like you are looking through a microscope lens.

    Focusing on what is in front of you. Behind the layers of the masks, you have gotten so good at wearing and covering, is the version you are unsure of. Remove them. Remove the mask you use with your family, acquaintances and real friends, work, school, church, and even yourself. What do you see? Is it a true reflection of what is or what was? Are you taking in false evidence appearing real?

    Without blinking, your stare intensifies so much that your tunnel vision has activated. On most days, that tunnel has become so dark that there is no reflection of light. Not even a little spark. The twinkle of light that would shimmer now and again has dimmed to the finest needlepoint.

Instead of moving forward to a place where you can see your growth, the flashbacks of the little girl that you used to be, the little girl that didn't have a care in the world comes flooding your mind. You had such a fabulous imagination when you were younger. You had such boldness that you could be anything in this world and would succeed no matter what. Like a dark cloud that comes out of nowhere, full of rain busting at the seams, surrounded by booming sounds of thunder, it shakes you from the core. As the quick flash of lightning strikes every few minutes, the flashbacks start to feel like your reality.

    Similar to others, you had to grow up so fast and quickly. You made adult decisions and took on the responsibilities of the people who should have been protecting you. Hearing who and what you will become regardless of your wants and dreams.

    As the feeling of frustration, anger, and self-doubt start to boil up in your gut like a volcano, your eyes become glossy and start to fill up with tears to the brim. You start taking deep breaths and inhale. Counting 1, 2, 3, 4, and 5 then exhale. Your breath is so ragged that you know your tears are about to flow down, but you refuse to give in. Inhaling again, 1, 2, 3, and 4. Just before you can get to 5 that teardrop on the corner of your eyelid is about to betray you as so many have. You're about to give up and let the waterworks begin. You have been strong for so long. That kick butt and take names attitude kicks in. You tell yourself there's no time to have a pity party. You have to get ready.

You jump in the shower and begin washing away every feeling and thought that had just bombarded your mind and was about to overtake you. You take your body wash and scrub away those feelings of unworthiness, self-doubt, not good enough, not feeling pretty enough, or how you wish this was not the texture of your hair and your skin's complexion. Just like the hot water washes away, you remind yourself that what you have been through has made you stronger. Most females in a similar or even worse situation would have thrown in the towel and waved the white flag to surrender because they can't take it. You replay in your head an inspiration reel you saw on IG last week and say to yourself,

"You are no longer a victim because you have pressed towards being a VICTOR!"

You take a deep breath. Inhale in and exhale out and get ready to put on the mask that you have become accustomed to wearing around others. Alexa, play "Brown Skin Girl" by Beyonce [1] on volume 10. Even though it doesn't change what you have endured, you pick out your cutest outfit,

---

[1] Beyonce. *"Brown Skin Girl"*. The Lion King: The Gift. July 19, 2019

diva lashes, lip gloss, and that bubbly persona with a smile on the side.

"Alexa, what's the temperature today?"

"It is 60 degrees today with a bit of sunshine."

You think to yourself, what should I wear? It will be a big day, but you are not feeling up to it. But they say if you look good, then you'll feel good. So let's take inventory. One must self-examine. You go into your closet and looking through the shirts, jeans, dresses, and jumpsuits you have on the hangers. You cannot and will not be able to know yourself until you take the time to be still and sit with yourself. No distractions, outside influences, no social media, just me, myself and I.

Many people don't know themselves because that sort of silence scares them. It's too uncomfortable to be alone with every flaw staring back at you. It is in the uncomfortable places that things manifest. It is not until you are alone, evaluating, and completely truthful with yourself that you will be able to see every facet of your life. The good, the bad and the ugly all make you the woman you are today.

In the quietness of being still, I tend to start talking to myself about how sick and tired I am of things, and the likely person to blame is God. What if for a moment I closed my mouth and just took inventory? Chalmers Brothers has a quote that *"Observing yourself is the necessary starting point for any real change."* Are you ready for real change? Are you ready to realize who you truly are and not who you want to be? I tend to already have a set idea of who I desperately want to be. It might not be whom I am designed to be. That's why knowing who you are is so important. When you know who you are, you won't need a person to tell you who you are.

Getting ready is always a process because it's meant to prepare you for what lies ahead of you. You can only be a prisoner to things if you allow them to control you. So here are a few things to assist you with *"getting ready"*.

Things To Remember:
Find what you are good at (and not good at). It's like finding the perfect shoes or an accessory.

This might be the most challenging step in discovering who you are, but it's necessary. Sure, it takes trial and error to find what you're good at. I don't want you to give up before you've had more than enough attempts but knowing when to stop is a gift that everyone needs to learn. Evacuate the situation or relationship when you have put in the time and your efforts are not giving you back a return.

What is ample time? Only you can decide that. But quitting correctly isn't giving up; it's making room for something better. When your actions do nothing but drain you rather than produce more passion and increase your drive to do more, that is not a good sign. It means it is time to focus elsewhere. Your strengths will show you who you are.

Find what you are passionate about.

What are you packing in your bag? What *"coat"* are you putting on? What are you willing to leave behind? Following your passion is a good thing, and you need to pay attention because it indicates an area of your life that you need to pay more attention to. Understanding yourself first makes a more significant impact. Passion produces effort, and continuous effort produces results.

Assess your WORTH: Now you are looking in a full-body mirror.

A prominent aspect of knowing yourself can be found in your relationships. When you realize you'll never honestly know anyone else until you discover yourself, the importance of knowing yourself becomes even more apparent. As much as you need to know yourself, others also need to know who you are. People need you—the real you.

When you understand whom you are meant to be, your purpose will finally become bigger than your fears. You will spend less time spinning your wheels when you realize who you are. Focusing on your strengths gives you the needed traction to make an effective difference. When you know yourself, you will find more peace and success quicker. Now go take action and find your true self. Starting today.

Ask for feedback. Take inventory of yourself first, and then ask others.

Hearing what others say about you is a helpful practice if you don't know yourself. Ask them two simple questions:

1. What strengths do you think I need to develop further?
2. What weaknesses do you think I need to work on?

Of course, their opinion isn't perfect. Their feedback will probably indicate a few areas you should at least take a second look at. This step is crucial for those who are stuck in finding themselves. Sometimes those closest to us can see something we might not be able to see in ourselves.

Chapter 2

Path-Less Traveled

In life, I must decide what I want. It's no longer a "fake it until I make it." I need reinforcements to get through the ups, downs, and self-doubt.

It's true that living with regret can be incredibly challenging. The struggle often stems from our desire to control outcomes and our natural inclination to second-guess ourselves. We want to believe that every choice we make is the best one, but life is full of uncertainties and complexities that make it impossible to know with absolute certainty.

One way to approach this is to remember that regret is a natural part of the human experience. It's a sign that you're reflecting on your choices and their consequences, which can be a source of growth and learning. When you look back and question your decisions, you're engaging in a process that can help you understand yourself better and make more informed choices in the future.

Embracing your choices involves accepting that you made the best decision you could with the information and perspective you had at the time. It's about recognizing that every decision, whether it leads to a positive outcome or not, contributes to who you are and who you are becoming. By doing so, you acknowledge your agency and autonomy, and you honor your journey, including its mistakes and successes.

The challenge often lies in reconciling your past decisions with your present self. It can be helpful to focus on self-compassion and understanding. Instead of dwelling on what could have been, you might find it useful to ask yourself what you can learn from the experience and how you can apply that wisdom going forward.

Ultimately, the conversation with yourself is about finding peace and acceptance. It's about understanding that life is a continuous process of growth and that every experience, including regret, can lead to deeper insight and personal development.

Imagine that you are on this path and arrive at a fork in the road. This fork in the road is between your current state and your *"there"* state. The *"there"* state is where you desire to be, by any means necessary. It is the point where once you get there, you will feel accomplished and think, I have finally arrived at the place that has always felt like a dream that was unattainable.

This is a road that you have been traveling down for several years. It's been a bumpy road, and sometimes it's been smooth. You cannot always predict when a situation will arise. Even though you have traveled down this road so often, you should know every bump, hole, debris, construction area and exit. Each time it has you wondering how long you will keep this up. How long are you going to keep letting life happen to you?

As you get this epiphany, you approach this fork in the middle of the road. You can either go right or left. You don't know where either road will take you, but you know that you cannot continue living life the way you have been living. You are sick and tired of being sick and tired. So you have two options ahead of you. A decision must be made and time is of the essence.

Why does it have to be black or white? Several things can have gray areas, but it's always two options. The hearers and the doers. Right or wrong. Pain or pleasure. Happy or sad. Left or right. Should I call/text or should I not? It's decision after decision and I do not know about you but I am over it.

I am over worrying if the choices I am making are going to have a consequence or pull me back 6 steps. So I start to question if this was reality or if I have made these things up in my head. Have I lost touch with reality because this can't be life, right? Do I have to make life-altering decisions that I am not even sure are best for me? The person I am today will not be who I will be in 6 months or even a year.

When I sit still by myself with no music or TV, I begin to talk to myself out loud. We all do it even if it is only a back-and-forth conversation in your head. I realize that as much as I feel conflicted I have to make some life-changing decisions. Being stagnant is no longer acceptable for me. I say that because of my obedience and coming into an agreement with whom I am becoming in this season of my life, and it's not that bad.

Seeing the path less traveled is where I was drawn to but only because I have now overanalyzed, second-guessing and taking this self-inflicted emotional roller coaster. Thank God I do not look like what I have been through. Losing touch with what is happening right in front of me is scary and happens more often than not. Society, especially social media, has subliminally convinced us that it's all about what looks good regardless of it being real or fake. I think about when I was younger and had all these dreams that I would achieve all these great and magnificent things. I operated in a space of pure innocence where there was unsolicited, no-limit, blinding faith. It was an intense feeling that caused me to block out any and everything and focus. No distraction or temptation could intervene. I was determined to soar farther than anyone else that I knew. I woke up every day declaring things over my life without truly knowing the power in my tongue.

I would speak about how I would:

- go to school and get good grades
- go to college
- become an entrepreneur
- get a successful high-paying career
- become a homeowner
- get married
- have 6 kids
- travel the world
- retire at 65 years old
- be my own boss and not work for anyone

Sounds simple enough, right? Wrong! Real life happens to us and it may cause a detour from the *plan* which now has us on a football field when we started on home plate at a baseball field. As a result choosing the path that many have traveled can be deemed as the less challenging because who wants to struggle right? Wrong again! Taking the most convenient or normal route will lead you to no fulfillment, restlessness, or keep you going in circles like a hamster on a wheel. A wheel which creates cycles.

This approach causes one to be on autopilot or stuck in a sunken place. Regardless if it is good or bad when things happen a response kicks in. Like most folks, we avoid them, flee and do not deal with them, or fight without the necessary resources or tools needed. As a result, we have become numb or do not know how to respond and absorb the impact. Even a pilot must come off of autopilot when turbulence hits.

Traveling as a whole can be exciting or draining but we have to be full participators in the experience. I would say that I am a serial traveler. Each time I go somewhere new or revisit a place I receive a new revelation. One that I received while traveling to New York City blessed me, and I hope it will do the same for you.

I was heading across the George Washington Bridge and it dawned on me how bridges have a special place in transportation infrastructure due to their direct relationship with other places. These structures have the purpose to carry on the traffic loads of the highway, crossing any obstacle, and performing effective communication between two destinations. There will be things that will cause you to get from one place to the next because it connects (*bridges*) you from your past to your future. But when you are dealing with a road it can be dangerous because you will go up and down that road that will cause you into a holding pattern that you can't break.

There will be a journey that we all will travel designed directly for us and where we are going in life. We will all take different modes of transportation and routes to get there based on our individual needs and convenience. Just like that journey, taking the highway or the back roads is up to you.

As I would say, I am a lifelong learner and partaker on a never-ending quest to reach my fullest potential. There are times that I need to think outside of my *"BUT"* and question my own B.S. (belief systems) which is a continuous thing. I strive to be the best version of myself. I cannot say to my mentees that we need to be the change we want to see and then punk out when the adversary hits. I must put pressure on my purpose and trust me, it is an uphill battle daily. I may make it look easy, but it is no easy task. I remind myself that I just need to take it one moment at a time and encourage myself, especially when I have to make decisions and believe.

I am unstoppable and I don't need permission to embrace my greatness. Even when I am afraid, I often do it anyway. I am the master of my destiny, with the help of God, of course. I want you to know that as you face each day, stand on that tiptoe anticipation that you are going to take on this journey and be excited doing it.

"This is the day the Lord has made; We will rejoice and be glad in it". [2]

Weigh your options. First, identify the Goal. Think about what you want to achieve. What do you want your outcome to be? Once you have made that decision, and then come to an agreement that you will see it through to the end regardless of the obstacles. Just like we learned in school, set SMART (*specific, measurable, attainable, relevant, and time-bound*) goals. Take baby steps, it is needed! If you take your bigger goals and break them down into smaller ones, then it will allow you to stay motivated and committed throughout the process. This will also limit the feeling of being overwhelmed or anxious.

Secondly, set standards. You should always strive to be the best version of yourself. Know that it is a process. Give yourself some grace and focus on being better than you were the day before. Hence, you no longer tolerate certain habits or character traits that do not serve you. It manifests in how you carry yourself every day and what you do consistently.

Third, be aware. Fourth, take your time. People make poor choices when in a bad mood or under much stress. When faced with a decision, it's ok to take a

---

[2] *www.biblegateway.com Psalms 118:24 (NKJV)*

moment to breathe, gather the information you have in front of you and then take a break. Go for a walk, pray, spend half an hour meditating, nap, or have a glass of wine.

The idea is to give your unconscious mind some time to do what it does best. Your decision afterward is more likely to be the right, or at least a perfectly acceptable, one. Finally, self-reflect. After each decision, ask yourself how you felt afterward and what about the experience you can apply in the future.

Chapter 3
You Have Arrived!

It was not an easy task. I made it this far, so there is no turning back.

I have to live with the decisions that I have made regardless of the outcome. They say I should not live in regret. You know what? I shouldn't! I have to forgive and it starts with me. I beg you to forgive yourself. I know it is easier said than done, but I need you to let go and forgive yourself for your choices. You made those decisions based on what you believed were the best choice for you at that moment.

Life is not fair. At my age I had to arrive at a place where I have to live it out even if it is not ideal. I tend to get stuck in this pattern and become so hesitant that I cannot operate. I have realized that my hesitation is in my history and not my ability. If I could get past that then I can manifest into a sight to behold. I am living in the true, unapologetically and genuine space that I have been striving and praying for.

I think about one of my lowest times. I arrived at a point in my life where there was no turning back. Have you heard the saying, *"what you don't confront, you will conform to?"* Well that is a true statement. I was (past tense) a victim of not just one but TWO abusive relationships. It was easy for me to succumb to this toxic cycle because some things were not dealt with in my childhood. I suppressed it and during my teenage years, those issues attempted to resurface. I continued to suppress them more and more until I went to therapy and did the work.

Every little girl desires to be daddy's little girl. When you get a taste of it, you believe there is no greater feeling. You embrace it and learn the feeling of protection, security, and love. You look forward to stepping on your daddy's feet while he teaches you the waltz, and all you can anticipate is the spin. You know it will consist of three turns and then a dip. You don't even care that you will have a short dizzy spell because you are with the first man you were taught to love. The man that always had a full battery charged on his VHS video camera at every recital and school play. The man that would make you hot tea and toast with cheese every morning and a trip to McDonald's or Dunkin Donuts after school.

I had plenty of great moments with my dad growing up. Even when times were not so great he was right there in front making sure no harm came my way. I thought there was no better way to live life. Even through the bad times, I thought the good and bad would cancel each other out. They did not! It took over twenty five years, therapy and a conversation with my dad to finally come to terms with it.

One memory that stands out was when I was in elementary school. There was a father-daughter dance that my father escorted me to. My hair was done in my dad's favorite hairstyle; two ponytails braided to the end with barrettes. I wore a floral dress that fell just below my knees. I had on ankle lace socks and patent leather shoes. They were so shiny you could see your face. My mother even let me wear my Guyanese gold earrings, necklace and bracelet. You would have thought I was heading to church on Easter Sunday.

I was in route to the father-daughter dance with my leading man in tow. I walked into that gymnasium with the biggest smile as I looked out to the crowd and saw my friends with their dads and father figures. It was a beautiful sight. All that mattered was that my dad was there. I already knew I was going to kill it on the dance floor because dancing was me and my daddy's favorite thing to do. I was going to share it with others. I don't remember how many songs I danced to with my friends or what the punch and hors d'oeuvres tasted like but I know I had a lot of energy that night. I remember as the time passed I was giggling with the Fly Girlz. The Fly Girlz was my group of girlfriends and most of us had been friends since pre-k or kindergarten. I remember while in mid-laugh I realized that my dad was nowhere to be found.

    Initially it did not bother me because I was partying with my Fly Girlz, which was always fun. Lord knows I did not want to miss anything, so I enjoyed the rest of the dance. At the end of the dance is when it got real. I ended up going home with my friend's father. The entire ride home I kept thinking how I was beyond angry at my dad. I kept thinking about how we did not get to dance and show off our skills and triple spins. I wanted to cry but I wasn't going to. I couldn't let my friend, or her dad see how upset I was. God forbid I told my family's business to *"strangers"* (anyone outside of the people I lived with). I buried every bit of lipid (oil), water, and mucus and refused to let one tear drop fall. I had mustered all the strength and energy I had to put on a smile until I got home and was laying in my bed. How can the man that said he loved me abandon me like that. Especially on such an important night for a little girl!

    I laid in the bed with arms crossed over my chest, my face was puffed out like a blowfish, and my nostrils were flared up as high as I could get them. I was determined to stay like that until he came home and checked on me and my sisters like he did every night and every morning before going to work.

Knowing how I was raised one would think *"Oh it's going down when I get home because my mommy is going to have a fit,"* but that was not the case. My mom raised all three of her daughters to be vocal and speak up about any and everything but do it respectfully. How could I? How could I tell my mom that my dad left me at the dance to hang out with his friends? I did not want my mom to be mad at my dad because even though I was hurt by it, I did not want me or anyone else to be mad at him. He had never done anything like that before.

In that pre-adolescent mind of mine, I tried to make sense of it and concluded that I was being selfish. I was wrong for holding this one thing against my first love. I sucked it up and buried the hurt and feelings deep down. It was hard to acknowledge that my superhero let me down. He made sure I had a roof over my head, food in my stomach and clothes on my back.

A couple of years after the dance, I was molested by an uncle in the kitchen while getting food out of the refrigerator for a block party. I remembered the following day while gripping my cousin's hand so tight, I told my mom what happened at the block party. She called my dad and told him to come home right away. Before I could even process what was happening, my daddy was there in a flash, running up the stairs to my room. I explained what happened again and my parents were furious. Especially my dad. My parents told us all to get dressed and get in the car. The superhero I had known and loved was in full effect, cape and all.

    He and my mother took me back to the house where it happened and were ready to raise hell and put folks on notice. The hurt I felt at that father and daughter dance kept getting buried further down because the good outweighed the bad. Even in my *"rebellious"* teenage moments of being rude and talking back, the root of that anger came from the hurt of that father-daughter dance. I continued to act out and felt justified in my actions because of that hurt that I felt so many years ago. It was never addressed or dealt with until my adult years.

    In my late teens and early 20's, there were so many red flags. They were flying so high but I overlooked them because, just like a child, I started to do the math. The good was greater than the bad. There's no need to address the issue or so I thought.

    That is the wrong approach and a toxic equation. The philosophy behind that thinking may work in certain instances, but it depends on the situation. It should be an exception and not the rule. When you have done the work, the equation changes. As a young woman, I was raised to be strong and independent and not let any man put their hands on me.

Like the rapper Eve said, *"Love is Blind"*[3]. It can be blind. Especially when pieces of yourself have not been addressed or healed. There are many forms of abuse; physical, sexual, psychological, emotional, mental, and financial, to name a few. Most people will tell you, just leave. When you are in that situation, it's not always that easy. The trauma that you have experienced lasts longer than the bruises.

I remember being ashamed that I was a victim not once but twice. I endured some labor pains but what was birthed out of it has forever changed me and allows me to be no longer bound to my young self that wanted to keep face but a conqueror of my past. I learned to trust that I deserve to be loved and protected.

When I dealt with my trauma in therapy is where the realization came. I learned that my dad dropped the ball and it was not my place as the child to rationalize or justify the actions of an adult. It also was not my

---

[3] Eve. Love is blind. *Let there be Eve…Ruff Ryders' First Lady.* August 31, 1999

responsibility to self-soothe or suppress my feelings so that others could feel better about themselves.

During my healing process, I learned how to not only navigate through uncomfortable places and situations but how to be in touch with my feelings and practice healthy coping skills. I learned to manage and deal with each thing continuously because it is not a one-time fix. It is all about trusting the process.

I remember when I first heard that statement it made me cringe. Thankfully, with prayer, time, and energy, along with preparation to have tough conversations with loved ones, friends, and foes, speaking engagements, sermons and writing this book, it has allowed me to grasp the concept fully. Don't rush the process. Trust it.
If things went the way I wanted them to, I would have accomplished some stuff and been on a different trajectory. The result would have been different and would not have been as good. God's timeline is being enforced as I "trust the process." I am reaping and benefiting from it because I said yes. Yes I will trust the process. Yes, I will heal. Yes, I will wait on you and what I have gained, my God.
The expansion that is coming because I was broken, I can't say it was gracefully broken because it was not always graceful. Still, the generational curses and yokes that have

been broken and destroyed are not just for me but those that will come behind me. The deliverance and healing that came from finally having a conversation with my dad, MY GOD!

I remember like it was yesterday, I was on one of my many daily phone calls with my mom. I was telling her how I was having a conversation with some of my inner circle folks. I shared about how I was hurt by my father.

Mommy: Well, good thing you had the conversation with your father.

Me: What conversation? I did not say anything to him!

Mommy: Wait, when you were down here, I thought you were going to tell him since you are writing about him in the book.

Me: Uhhh no, we were having such a great time and talking about my childhood I didn't want to ruin it. I should just FaceTime him now and tell him. Do you think I should?

Mommy: I think you should.

Me: Alright, I'm going to call you back; I love you!

I took two DEEP and much needed breaths and then video called my daddy. Instantly I felt like that little girl with pigtails and a puffy floral dress. At that moment, it felt like time stood still. I was hoping that he would not pick up because I was beyond nervous to have this conversation. There was no turning back because he picked up.

> **Daddy:** *"How can I help you, Rohesia?"*
>
> **Me:** *Daddy, do you remember the Father & Daughter dance at Harriet Tubman Elementary School when I was younger?*
>
> **Daddy:** *Of course, I was actually thinking about it a few days ago. Matter of fact, I always think about that night from time to time.*
>
> **Me:** *Oh, well, do you recall how you left me that night and I had to get a ride home?*
>
> **Daddy:** *You did not get a ride home. I went to your uncle's house for a beer because it was so boring but when I got back, the dance was over.*
>
> **Me:** *Wait, what?! You did not come back, I got a ride home from a friend's dad.*
>
> **Daddy:** *(chuckling) Uh no, I was sitting there while you were dancing, talking to one of the fathers, and I was bored, so I left thinking that I could go and come back, but when I returned, the dance was over, and boy were you mad! You were puffed up with your nose flared, and we went home.*

Me: Omgeeeeee, you are kidding me. All this time, I thought you left me to hang out with your friends, and I had to get a ride from someone else. Shoot, I wish I knew that before this, then I would have saved a lot of money in therapy.

Daddy: Are you serious?!

Me: Yes, very serious. I talked about other things, but that father-daughter dance was a traumatic experience for me. I felt justified in my actions and outbursts during my teenage years because of that dance, and now that I know what happened and we have spoken, I feel like a giant weight has lifted off of me. Geez, I wished I would have said something sooner.

My dad and I spoke for a while longer. To summarize it, speaking to my father was very therapeutic and so needed. For years before therapy, I had this present dad whom I often bumped heads and would argue with constantly. Because he was physically and financially in my life I equated that to him loving me. After several heart-to-heart conversations with my daddy, since that day, not only do I now understand his love language, he understands mine as well.

To have him open up his emotions about being a girl dad and how he viewed his role as a dad has given me so much clarity. I may not have always agreed with my dad's method. However, I can understand how he did the best he could with the knowledge and resources he had. My father is a West Indian man (GT!!), brother to sixteen siblings and has a limited education. He married a vocal wife and had three daughters.

I didn't know how having this conversation would end or if it would bring up problems, but it was one of the best decisions I have ever made. It allowed me to face the brokenness I have felt for years and be made whole again. It doesn't change the fact that there are cracks that can be seen. The healing that has taken place allows me to see the cracks and use the experience to attack any problem or situation head-on. It was a lesson learned. Our relationship is still growing and glowing, but it is not where it used to be. I am beyond blessed to be one of the daughters of Mr. Lennox Hicks.

In life we will arrive at a point in our life that because of trauma or past experiences we will make a decision that will alter our lives for the good or the bad. If we remain in that "place" healing will not be able to take place so here is a simple as 1, 2, 3, and a bonus wink process.

1. Close your mouth, don't speak.
2. Physically remove yourself from that current space.
3. Take a deep breath.
4. Release the feeling by venting in a safe place with good counsel or a therapist.

Doing these steps in that order will allow you to start the healing process and not be triggered by the person/thing when you do return to that environment because you are dealing with the root of the problem.

Chapter 4

Ring My "Belle"!

Attention has been commanded in a crowded room because your presence has set the temperature similar to a thermostat.

My parents have always told me that there was something about me that was not like others. They did not know how to verbalize what that "it" factor was, but they knew it was special. It all started from the day I was born; on April 22nd at 12:06 pm. A precious little girl was born. I caught the attention of many nurses, residents, and doctors before I could even have my first cry. I think the story of my delivery is very comical, even though my mom disagrees.

She was on full display because I wanted to have a bowel movement before she pushed me out. Every year since I can remember, I call my parents 24 hours before my birthday and ask them to tell me what they were doing at this very moment back then. They tell me a play-by-play of every detail until my arrival against their will. As much as it annoys them, you would think I would not ask anymore but I still do!

When I think about my childhood and what I experienced, *"life for me ain't been no crystal stair"* (for all my Harriet Tubman Elementary School heads that had to learn Mother to Son by Langston Hughes) but I have arrived. I am one of three daughters from immigrant parents. Parents that wanted to ensure their children would have more than they did. I was named Rohesia, pronounced

Row-he-sha. My mom found my name in a baby book in London (that's right, the United Kingdom), which means rose.

My family always laughs when they recall when I was old enough to talk and say my name. They told me I was so proud to introduce myself to others. I would stand flat-footed, shoulders back, and head held high. Even though I had to constantly teach people how to pronounce my name, and still do to this day, you could not tell this little girl that her name was not a badge of honor. Nor that it would be in people's mouths for years to come and may even be in bright lights one day. Like anything in life, experiences and situations will cause you to question and rethink a lot.

Between being bullied for having more meat on my bones than the other girls and my name having an *"esha"* in it, people had already determined stereotypes about who I was. I could not fully grasp why. It has played such a heavy role in my life that it has dictated how I have shown up in spaces and places.

I was a first-generation, middle-class (although the government labeled me as low-income) black girl born in England. I was raised in Newark, NJ, right off of South Orange Avenue. This alone did not give me the boost of confidence that I needed at a time when my peers were always judging me. They would tell me I was *"ghetto"* and probably lived in the "projects" with "mad siblings" because of my name. Because of those and many more negative assumptions, I would dim my light around others. I would battle with what I did not have or could not do when I compared myself to others. I was so upset and ashamed that I was different from my peers.

    I remember coming home one day and being upset that we owned a house and car, took family vacations regularly on an airplane. I was upset that even when we argued it would be short lived because love would always overpower the issue. I came in the house yelling in full tantrum mode telling my mom that she did not love me and if she did then she would have never did this to me. How could you name me Rohesia? It is so hood and *"ghetto!"*

    I find it hilarious when I think back to those dramatic conversations I would have about how I would change my name to a simple and common name. At that adolescent stage, I could not see the courageous, bold and fierce girl I used to be. I did not know what I know now. Living through experiences and trauma has a way of shifting your perspective. It could be good if it is used as a learning experience or fuel to push you full steam ahead.

However, it can also be bad if you do what I did. I allowed the bad experiences to alter how I saw and showed up for myself, especially in spaces I did not feel adequate to be in.

Growing up, I would say that I was a chunky old thing. I remember my ROD threatening to beat up the boys that made fun of me because of my weight. She would remind me of all the fantastic things I had to offer and tell the bullies,

> "That's all you got? My friend is cute, has long hair, and doesn't stink."

My ROD would say it with so much conviction that I believed every word. My posture would change after she told them off. I would take a deep breath and walk around school like I was a model on a runway.

The vibe I gave off was that this girl was super confident. It didn't matter what was said because she knew who she was and her best friend would beat you up. I laugh to myself because even after over thirty years, my ROD is still the same way about me. She is even more protective.

At that young age, I would get pushed down but rise every time with more fierceness than before. I did not allow anything or anyone to stop me from shining my light very brightly. All that changed as I got older. Even to this day, I still struggle with it. Some days are better than others, but that imposter syndrome kicks in super hard. Imposter syndrome is a persistent internal feeling of inadequacy regardless of whether you are killing the game and achieving greatness externally.

    I think this condition started around middle school for me. I was told I would not be more than a hood girl that would not go to college, let alone graduate high school. I was told I would either be locked up, a single mother with multiple children by different men or find myself six feet under.

    Now that was just one side of the balancing scale. On the other side, society tells me that it's different for a black girl or woman. I have to be better than the others. I have to have it all together and be humble so I am not seen as threatening. While doing that I needed to be married and *"pop out"* a few kids. It is a repeated cycle of how others are seen as your competition. You must be the best of the best!

Don't get me wrong, I believed both things and fought hard not to be a statistic even though I felt I had a disadvantage. I strived to be the best but it was so dysfunctional. Instead of wanting to be better than my peers, I would feel that I wasn't good enough and compare myself to others every chance I got.

I decided to prove myself worthy by getting so career driven that I would sign myself up to be a part of opportunities to get a leg up on others. No matter how overwhelming or draining it was. It is not bad to be ambitious, but when your WHY is not fully developed, or you cannot fully articulate it, you are in serious trouble. This way of thinking had me showing up at meetings, events and jobs striving to figure out if I belonged or how to "fake it until I make it." That was a way of life for me until during one of my therapy sessions I realized that I needed to identify a mentor that could guide, advise and assist me with navigating not only my career but personally too.

When identifying who will mentor you, you should not take it lightly. There are many things to consider.

- The mentee will supersede their mentors.
- The mentees ask to be mentored.
- The mentor is not your friend.
- The mentor sees where you are going not where you are currently.

I also learned and realized, while talking to my therapist, that it was ME telling myself, not people, that I don't belong at the tables that I kept finding myself at because I didn't look or sound like those around me. I feel as though society has convinced me to believe that I have to have it all together but also be set apart from others in the same breath. Nothing can have control over me unless I allow it. When things feel like it is all over the place, I recall that only I can control the controllable.

As I am continuing to build my self-worth and value, I have come to the realization that there may still be times when the "imposter syndrome" may arise but utilizing the steps below allows for that feeling to be temporary and short-lived. I also stay in remembrance of my constant prayer:

> *"Lord, I thank you for the opportunities that are ahead of me and I asked that you will allow my name to be in spaces and places that my feet have not entered yet. That my name will be on people's mouths and minds when greater is an opportunity for me and I thank you in advance for the abundance of elevation, expansion, greater territory, and resources that will pour over me."* Amen.

Separate feelings from facts. Be ready for those feelings of imposter syndrome to creep in. Do not focus on the feeling but observe. Be mindful and ready to respond. It is just a thought and does not mean it is true.

Celebrate the small wins! Take note of your accomplishments no matter how big or small they are. Be sure to hang up your certificates, diplomas and degrees. If you see it then you have no choice but to believe that you are winning.

Stop comparing! That type of behavior is self-destructive. It will rob you of peace and joy. When we stop comparing ourselves to others, we run our own race at our own pace. At the end of the day it is about your journey within yourself.

Talk to others. Have a good chat with *"good counsel."* Someone who knows you, is not moved by your attitude and is okay with you never speaking to them again can help you realize that your imposter feelings are irrational but normal.

Talk to a therapist. A therapist can help you identify the feelings associated with the imposter syndrome and develop and create healthy behaviors to get you to take action and move forward.

Chapter 5

Was It All a Dream?

It seems too good to be true that one cannot identify if it was real or a dream. Can the vision manifest?

I am a true believer that there is power in my tongue and that it will manifest if I am strategic and intentional. It is about putting in the work even when the odds are against me. It's about doing it afraid with power and persistence when all others have doubted me. With that kind of strength, I have learned it will come to fruition. Several keys are needed to bring forth the manifestation one seeks. I will talk about vision, which has taken me a few years to fully grasp. It's not just about what God or others see for me. It's about agreeing with what is being seen and believing it is for me regardless of my circumstance because I deserve greatness.

Past situations have taught me that God will give me more than I can ask, think or feel I can manage. Knowing what lies ahead of me or where I should be is way too small for what I have been purposed to do. To really and truly know the manifestation of the things I will accomplish, I need to identify sight. Not just any type of sight but insight. Insight is being crazy enough to believe that even though I do not see it, God's perspective is right on the money.
Seeing and focusing on what is right in front of me is the lowest level of perspective. Let's think about it. If I focus on what is right before me, the here and now will be altered

based on the current situation or circumstance. Depending on what lens I am looking out of will determine if I believe this too shall pass and if it is only temporary. I need to be pinched because this must be a dream because my reality is telling me differently.

    I recall many out-of-reality moments when I felt like I did not recognize anything or even myself. How could I have a supportive circle, money in my bank account (not just one but two accounts), a job I enjoyed, opportunities and doors opening left and right? That is when it hit me that the scale was not balanced. What I thought was happening was different than what I was experiencing. Hence it is essential that I stop and think before responding or making a decision. If I can have a moment to pause and breathe before I speak, it will limit haste decisions. It is a significant problem when a decision is made based on my feelings, others or a situation that can be altered for good or bad in a blink of an eye.

    I am a visual person, and it is not only my learning style but also my lifestyle. I am a visionary. I can see the big picture and baby, it looks good! So if I can see it, then I can obtain it. The concern is not whether I can access what is right in front of me but what I do with what is given to me. When life gives you lemons what you do with it matters. Do you make lemonade to drink or create a bestselling album that will last a lifetime? It's all about what you make of the situation.

When you self-evaluate and reflect it allows you the opportunity to honestly acknowledge, accept and learn from the experience so that it can give you a framework to start with. There will be pros and cons that will come to mind so write them down so it is no longer in your head. They say a picture is worth a thousand words and it is true. If you are like me you see the end goal so clear but the steps that need to be taken seem all over the place. It's not, but our mind is always running a hundred miles a minute. Similar to when I create a vision board. After I have all the pictures and quotes I want and the board is looking full and pretty, I develop a priority list so I can focus on a few important things versus the whole board. Once I do that I realize that the things on my list actually build upon one another.

The bible tells us that we should, *"Write the vision and make it plain upon tablets, that he may run that readeth it."* [4] That is exactly what it is about. No time to over think or keep going back and forth. No matter how far-fetched it may seem, write it anyway.

---

[4] *www.biblegateway.com Habakkuk 2:2 (KJ21)*

When I decided to launch *Visions of Belle*, my girl's organization, it seemed like a wild stretch. I remember while sitting at a diner with my brother, I told him my plan to do a girls group and he said ok. We flipped over the paper menu and started writing the vision. So many people told me how crazy I was for doing this when I would talk about it. I recall being so angry that I posted the following message on social media:

> *"Ppl have been asking and saying to me why am I doing this? Why would you add something else to your plate? You're setting yourself up for failure because teen girls have the worst attitudes! Do you really want to deal with these girls and their issues because it can be deep? Do you really think you can make a difference w/them especially at that age group? My answer & response is simple.... ABSOLUTELY because if these young ladies only have women like you around then they are doomed so take notes and have a blessed day!"*

I did it anyway and seven years later, *Visions of Belle* is still going strong. We are expanding and elevating every year. Does it get tough? Absolutely! So, I continue to go back to my WHY and remember that I gave a YES not only to God and the young ladies I have and will impact and influence but also to myself. Over the years, people have let me down but the one constant person in all of this is ME. I will always show up for myself especially for the wildest of dreams.

Vision will precede the provision.

- Stop and Think
- Assess the Reality
- Write down the Pros & Cons
- Identify the Big Picture
- Write the Vision (Make it Plain)
- Prioritize what is Important!

Chapter 6
Where's My Return?

Every time I take two steps forward, I am brought back ten steps. Enough is enough. I have put in the work to become my best version and I will not allow a temporary situation to be withdrawn from me because I am demanding a return on my investment.

Over the years, I have learned how important it is to honor yourself. It is pretty simple when you think about it, especially when you are on the other side of that thing. When you honor something or someone you assess a value to it. Only you can determine that value because you have endured a cost that could have taken you out. But, you have back up. You have to determine what is essential to your life and how to remain focused on that even when the odds are against you.

Similar to when an emergency arises and we are told to please remain calm so that we can exit in an orderly manner, the same applies when a situation takes us back to a place we thought we had overcome. The most contradictory assistance I can offer is to remain calm. Do not put this book down just yet. Remember, this chapter is about a return on your investment, so listen closely. Like everyone else, I have endured many storms that took me over the edge or too close for comfort. However, the blessing was that I learned how to navigate the investment versus cost. In order to tackle this, you can be in your feelings or operate off of emotions to handle the situation. It takes maturity and obedience to do something much higher than oneself. For me, God is that one! He keeps me all the way together, especially when I want to respond as *"Roe-Roe"* from 2010.

Do I always get it right? No, because I am not perfect. Let me tell you, I am better than I was before. After I take a moment to let the present situation marinate by breathing, I then look at the cost versus the investment. In most cases, identifying and weighing the cost can take you into a tailspin. Especially when the analytical side is front and center. Cost requires a sacrifice, and usually, that sacrifice is something or someone you have become quite attached to. It can be deemed good or bad. This is why it's essential to do the math. Expenses will incur, but YOU get to decide the impact it will make.

How do you do that? Well, I use the arithmetic operations to decide if the return is worth the investment. I look to see if it adds, subtracts, multiplies, or divides to my life and the ultimate goal by asking myself follow-up questions:

- **Addition:** will it add to what I am already working towards? Will the sum of what I add be positive or negative? Will it be more significant now or later?
- **Subtraction:** will it take away from who I need to become? Will it remove something or

someone that is needed for my next level because of *blurred vision* I do not recognize?

- **Multiplication:** will it produce a GREATER outcome because the progression continues to multiply?
- **Division:** will it cause a separation? Will I be divided into smaller pieces and unable to become whole again?

When all is said and done, I have to ask myself, will it multiply to my desired quality of life? You may think I am too deep, but you might have to come away from that shallow end and dive in deeper. Here is a bonus example with some simplification.

If you had $100 and applied each operation by $100, which would you choose?

(a) $100 + $100 = $200

(b) $100 - $100 = $0

(c) $100 x $100 = $10,000

(d) $100 ÷ $100 = $1

It is so obvious, right? I am aiming for my return to be multiplied every time. I have and continue to do the work. I have done self-exploration, gone to therapy and continue to go to therapy. I have forgiven others as well as myself. I have and continue to pray, read books, seek good counsel, and let go and let God! This is not a quick fix and is a reoccurring cycle. More often than not it feels like every time I take two steps forward, I am being brought back ten steps.

There are moments when I am at rock bottom and unsure at what point I will be back on top. Sometimes I can barely keep my head above water, and several boats are in the vicinity, and I am attempting to figure out what boat will carry me to safety. Those moments cause an indescribable emotion of pain, hurt, sadness, doubt, and uncertainty.

I have to quiet the noise around me and even in my head to tell myself that this is temporary. It is temporary because I remember so many situations where I felt that this time it was over. I did not want to live through the seconds of the day and now I can stand years later stronger than ever.

I am here to tell you that you will get through whatever your *"IT"* is and be better for it. I cannot give you an expiration date but I can tell you what I did. It was simple. I surrendered it all! I gave myself, the situation, people, and the pain from my feelings and did not pick them back up. God turned it all around. I started seeing the positivity in the matter. I started smiling again and finding my joy.

A really good friend asked me, "What does joy look like for me?" I thought long and hard and couldn't answer that question. Months later, while driving to church one Sunday morning, it hit me like a ton of bricks. I realized that joy is not just a thing but an intense feeling or emotion. It will make the cloudiest day seem bright, and it is not temporary. Momentary things like happiness can be present even with the circumstances are not happy. We must learn how to continue to move those traumatic experiences through our bodies instead of being buried in our subconscious or hearts. That will turn into sickness. When we move, especially forward, there is no opportunity for anything to fester. If we go back to the basics that we learned watching those throwback black movies, they showed us a woman that we could relate to going through heartache and pain. Before their breakthrough there was some type of movement that would take place. Whether it was rocking back and forth with a face full of tears, or being sick and tired of being sick and tired. Those women never stopped striving to move forward even when all hope was lost.

We need to be able to access that joy and realize that nobody can take it away from us. Joy is an emotion that lives deep within us. We cannot always see or feel it. Often the bigger emotions, negative ones such as anger, hurt or sadness, take over because they seem very present in our daily life. That is when we have to protect our peace and continue to invest in ourselves at a higher rate.

Due to the deposit that was made on bended knees with blood soaked tears, it belongs to us and now all we have to do is access it. We have to give permission to our adult self that has been protecting our young self all these years that it is ok. We are ok and will be ok. I tell my Belles all the time opportunities only matter if we are positioned to receive and then access it.

- Remain Calm (1, 2, 3 Breathe with Me 3X)
- Do the Math
- Call it out
- Access it

Finale

If it is not written, it's not real. "I am" in Hebrew means and it came to pass so, let's manifest what will come!

I want you to take away a few things. Get ready to travel the path less traveled because that is where you will arrive. Be the "Belle of the Ball" that commands peace, boldness and joy. You will pass all understanding that it will feel like it was all a dream. Remember all these great things that are now manifesting in your life is just the return on your investment.

I love you and know that you too are the author of your story. Stand in front of that mirror and with power in your voice say the following "I AM" affirmations and it will come to pass!

I am brave.

I am happy to be here.

I am always learning.

I am an intelligent being.

I am proud of who I am.

I am happy.

I am responsible.

I am not in a race; there is plenty of time.

I am strong.

I am going to get through this.

I am unique.

I am patient.

I am worthy.

I am lovable.

I am fun.

I am creative.

I am trustworthy.

I am a survivor.

I am loved.

I am "me".

I am more than enough.

I am in complete control of my thoughts.

I am a unique.

I am fully capable of success.

I am worthy of love and appreciation.

I am forgiving myself for past mistakes.

I am at peace with my past.

I am surrounded by so much love.

I am responsible for the energy I put out into the world.

I am capable of attracting abundance daily.

I am grateful for what I do have in my life.

I am confident in myself and my ability to manifest a better life.

I am determined to attract happiness into my life.

I am stronger than I appear.

I am letting go of negative patterns.

I am committed to putting positive energy into the world.

I am blessed to have a family that loves me.

I am determined to be my healthiest self in mind, body, and spirit.

I am grateful to be alive.

I am ready to explore all my passions.

I am aligned with my higher purpose.

I am vibrant in both spirit and mind.

I am fully responsible for my happiness.

I am content with the relationships I have in my life.

I am grateful for each opportunity that comes my way.

I am a leader and will use my influence to inspire positivity.

I am attracting money and wealth into my life.

I am constantly expanding my belief in what is possible.

I am capable of achieving my goals with determination.

I am ready for all that is to come.

I am daring to be different and unapologetically myself.

I am self-assured.

I am proud of my life choices.

I am proud of the person I am becoming.

I am striving to be a better person every day.

I am a good role model to younger generations.

I am going to put some good into the world today.

I am open to letting love enter my life.

I am worthy of receiving love.

I am practicing self-love each day.

I am ever evolving and constantly learning.

I am comfortable in my skin.

I am free to grow at my own pace.

I am perfect just the way I am.

I am in control of my actions.

I am giving myself the love I deserve to have.

I am committed to taking my needs seriously.

I am listening to my gut.

I am letting my body heal.

I am forgiving myself and others.

I am releasing all negative energy that hurts me.

I am going to treat everyone the way I want to be treated.

I am trusting the journey ahead.

I am taking each day as it comes.

I am grateful for my immune system's ability to heal.

I am grateful for my body.

I am observing my emotions without attaching myself to them.

I am sending love and light to all beings on the earth, even those that have done me wrong.

I am grateful for the air in my lungs.

I am a powerful.

I am attracting the perfect career.

I am influential in my field of work or study.

I am prepared for all that is to come.

I am aware that my success has no limits.

I am open to all new experiences.

I am putting my health first.

I am complete on my own.

I am saying no without apology.

I am accountable.

I am believing that everything happens for a reason.

I am trusting of my abilities.

I am striving to be the best version of myself.

I am at peace with my imperfections.

I am changing what I can't accept & accepting what I can't change.

I am standing for what I believe in.

I am a reflection of my highest self.

I am beautiful both inside and out.

I am not going to compare myself to others.

I am choosing not to let anger control me.

I am doing my best.

I am seeing the glass half full.

I am the pilot of my own life.

I am tending to my needs.

I am a positive influence.

I am not defined by my worst decisions.

I am worthy of success.

I am my own best friend.

I am practicing compassion each day.

I am not going to judge myself.

I am inhaling positive energy and exhaling negativity.

Made in the USA
Middletown, DE
13 February 2025